Spotlight on Reading

Story Elements

Grades 1–2

Frank Schaffer

An imprint of Carson-Dellosa Publishing LLC
Greensboro, North Carolina

Credits

Cover and Interior Design: Van Harris
Development House: The Research Masters

Cover photo © 1995 PhotoDisc, Inc.

This book has been correlated to state, common core state, national, and Canadian provincial standards. Visit *www.carsondellosa.com* to search for and view its correlations to your standards

Frank Schaffer
An imprint of Carson-Dellosa Publishing LLC
PO Box 35665
Greensboro, NC 27425 USA
www.carsondellosa.com

ISBN 978-16-099-6492-4
01-335117784

About the Book

Story Elements is designed to introduce young readers and writers to tools that authors use as they create stories. The activities explore the concepts of character, setting, problem (conflict), and plot. The book is divided into sections for each concept. Within each section, the activities progress from easiest to more challenging. In addition, some exercises include fictional stories while others feature nonfiction text.

Once students have been introduced to these basic concepts, reinforce their understanding by identifying characters, settings, problems, and plots in stories shared during story time and in reading groups.

• •

Table of Contents

Name _____

Look at pictures from three stories. Answer a question about each story.

• •

Every story has characters.

A story character can be a or who runs and plays.

Or, a story character can be a or a _____ .

Maybe the character is a _____ or a _____ .

Sometimes, characters feel happy. Sometimes, they feel sad.
Reading about characters we like can be fun!

1. _____

   Who is this story about?

   three birds and a boy   three bears and a girl

2. _____

   Who is this story about?

   a woman   a man

3. _____

   Who is a character in this story?

   a girl and a wolf   a boy and a cat

Try This: On another sheet of paper draw your favorite character.

Happy or Sad?

How does the character feel? Draw a happy face or a sad face or both in the box.

Here Is My Story

Look at the pictures and circle the character's name. Underline the best title for each story.

1. Mark

   Lisa

   Ruff

Lisa Washes Dishes   Lisa Makes a Mask

2. Mark

   Lisa

   Ruff

Mark Flies a Kite   Mark Does Homework

3. Mark

   Lisa

   Ruff

Ruff Plays Catch   Ruff Finds a Bone

Try this: On another sheet of paper write a story about one of these characters.

Story Elements • CD-104556

The Hunters

Read the story. Circle a picture to answer each question.

 asked her for some . She packed the

 , some , and in her . She was going on a hunting

trip.  walked to the . was in the ,

too. He had a  . and wanted to find something to

show at . saw an . She drew the with

her and . saw a . He took a picture of the

 with his . shared her with . It was a

good day. They both found something. They both had fun on their hunt.

1. Who took the to the ?

2. Who had a ?

3. Who took a backpack to the ?

4. Who saw an ?

5. Who saw a ?

Name _____

Read each story. Cut out the pictures of the four characters. Glue the picture of each character next to the right story.

• •

1. He hopped out of the oven.

    He ran and ran as fast as he could.

    No one could catch him.

2. He climbed up and up the water spout.

    The rain fell and washed him out.

    Later, he climbed again.

3. She wanted to bake bread.

    She asked the other animals to help.

    No one would help her.

    But they all wanted to eat her bread!

4. He went out with his mother and father.

    They found a girl in their home when they came back.

    The little girl was sleeping in his bed.

Name _____

Each picture shows a character. The title of the first picture is "Sue Goes to the Store." Write titles for the other pictures.

• •

1. Sue Goes to the Store

2. _____

   _____

3. _____

   _____

4. _____

   _____

Try this: Choose one character.
Write a story about his or her day on another sheet of paper.

Kit and Kitten

Read the stories on this page and the next. Answer the questions about each story.

• •

   Tommy is a baby fox. A baby fox is called a kit. Tommy has red fur and lives with his mother in the woods. Their home is called a den. Tommy and his mother hunt for food to eat. Tommy loves to go hunting in the woods!

1. Who is Tommy?

    _____

    _____

2. Where does he live?

    _____

    _____

3. What does he love?

    _____

    _____

Name _____

Sally is a baby cat. A baby cat is called a kitten. Sally has yellow fur. She lives in a house with a family. The family feeds Sally and plays with her too. Sally loves to live with the family!

1. Who is Sally?

   _____

   _____

2. Where does she live?

   _____

   _____

3. What does she love?

   _____

   _____

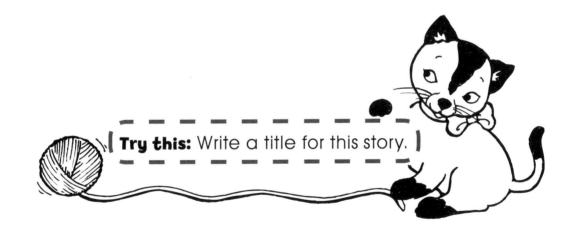

Try this: Write a title for this story.

Name _____

Read each sentence. Write the character's name on the line.

• •

1. "Hey! I am angry," said _____ .

2. "I am bored," said _____ .

3. "That loud noise scared me," said _____ .

4. "Mom and I are going to the beach," said _____ .

5. "I can't find my favorite toy," said _____ .

> **Try this:** On another sheet of paper write
> one more sentence for each character.

12

Time for Dusty

Read the story. Circle the correct answer to describe each character.

• •

Dusty wanted something. He ran to find Tyler. Tyler was reading a book. Dusty walked up the stairs to Holly's bedroom. She was playing a game. She did not look to see what Dusty wanted.

Dusty ran back down the steps. He picked up his leash. He took the leash and went to Tyler. This time, Tyler put his book down. "What do you want, boy?" Tyler asked.

Dusty ran to the door. He wagged his tail. So, Tyler pulled on his coat. He went to the steps and said, "Holly, do you want to go outside with us?"

"Yes," said Holly. She smiled.

1. Dusty

  boy   girl   dog

2. Tyler

  boy   girl   dog

3. Holly

  boy   girl   dog

┌ ─ ─ ─ ─ ─ ─ ─ ─ ─ ─ ─ ─ ─ ─ ─ ┐
Try This: On another sheet of paper draw a picture
of what might happen next.
└ ─ ─ ─ ─ ─ ─ ─ ─ ─ ─ ─ ─ ─ ─ ─ ┘

The Lion and the Mouse

Read the story. Answer the questions on the next page.

• •

Marta the Mouse squeaked as she ran through the jungle. "I love to run and play on such a beautiful day!" Suddenly, she heard someone cry out.

"Help! Can anyone help me?"

She ran toward the cries and found Leo the Lion. He had a thorn stuck in one of his legs.

"What's wrong, Leo?" Marta asked.

"I've got this thorn in my leg. But I can't pull it out. My paws are too big to grab it." Leo roared, "Oh, what will I do!"

"I'll help you, Leo," Marta replied.

"But you're a small mouse, Marta. How can you help a big lion?" Leo said.

"Just wait," Marta told him. "You'll see."

She reached for the small thorn. Leo's paws were too big to grab the thorn. But Marta's paws were just the right size.

She tugged and tugged. After a moment, the thorn came free.

"You did it!" Leo cried. "Thank you, Marta."

"See, Leo," Marta said. "You're never too small to lend a paw."

They laughed together.

Name _____

Circle an answer for each question. Use the Word Bank to write words or phrases that go with each character.

• •

Word Bank

big	small	tiny paws
roars	squeaks	big paws

1. What are the characters?

    kids   animals   cars

2. Are the characters real or make-believe?

    real   make-believe

3. Which character said, "I'll help you"?

    Leo   Marta

4. Which character said, "You did it!"

    Leo   Marta

5. Why did the lion cry out in the jungle?

    He needed help.   He was hungry.

6. Why did the mouse pull the thorn out?

    She was afraid of the lion.   She said she would help the lion.

Lion   _____   _____   _____

Mouse   _____   _____   _____

Name _____

Read about where stories happen. Use the pictures at the bottom of the page to answer the questions.

• •

The place a story happens is the **setting.** A setting can be a real place

like a  or a . Sometimes, the setting is make-believe.

A princess might live in a castle. A bird might live in a nest. A story about a bat

might take place in a cave. A story about a boy might take place in a park.

1. Draw a circle around the setting for a .

2. Draw a square around the setting for a .

3. Draw an X on the setting for a .

4. Draw a line under the setting for a .

Try this: Think about a story you like. Describe the setting on a separate sheet of paper.

In the Picture

Draw a setting around each character.

1.

2.

3.
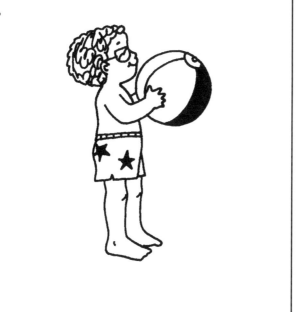

4.

Try this: On another sheet of paper draw another setting for one of these characters.

17

How Do You Feel?

The characters and settings in stories can make you feel happy or sad. Draw a line from each picture to how it makes you feel.

Happy

Sad

Try this: On another sheet of paper draw a setting that makes you feel happy.

Out of Place

Cross out the picture that does not belong in each setting.

• •

1.

2.

3.

4.

5.

19

Get the Picture

Choose words from the Word Bank. Write them on the lines under the setting where they belong.

• •

Word Bank

| bats | snow | water | stars | gate | trees |
| ball | rocket | ice | planets | towel | weeds |

1.

_____ _____

_____

2.

_____ _____

_____

3.

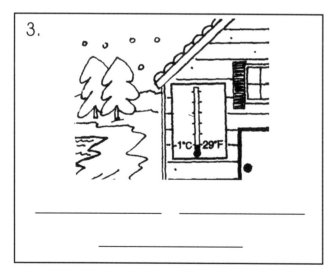

_____ _____

_____

4.

_____ _____

_____

Try this: Pick one setting. On another sheet of paper list three more things that belong there.

Do You Know the Time?

Sometimes, the setting tells us when the story takes place. Read each clue. Write the letter of the clues in the right months. The pictures can help you make matches.

• •

a. at a party, on a winter's night

b. in a field, making a snowman

c. in a yard, raking leaves

d. in a park, watching butterflies

e. on a beach, eating fruit

f. in a kitchen,
cutting pumpkin to bake a pie

Try this: Write a short story that takes place during one of these months.

Time Travel

Settings tell us if a story is set long ago, today, or in the future. Read each story sentence. When did each story take place? Draw an X in the right box.

	Long Ago	Today	Future
1. Josh saw the covered wagons roll across the plains. He liked living in the West.			
2. Tracy strapped on her helmet. She rode her bike along the trail.			
3. Mark looked at the stars around him. He lived in a green pod. He rode a rocket bus to school.			
4. It was Laura's first train ride. She watched the other wagons come to the station. The train left the station.			
5. Zach's family parked their mini-van in the big lot. They crossed a red bridge to the park.			

Try this: On another sheet of paper draw a picture to show one of these settings.

Story Elements • CD-104556

Name _____

Where Are We?

Read each paragraph. Choose the right setting from the Word Bank. Write the setting on the line under each story.

```
                         Word Bank

    school            outer space            forest
```

1. Chester was hungry. He ran down the tree trunk. He pawed at the dead leaves. He wanted the nut he had hidden yesterday. He dug and dug. It was not there! He looked at all the other trees. Now, where did he hide that nut?

_____

2. Miguel looked out the window. He could see Earth behind him. It looked very small from way out here. Then he looked at Pluto. That is where he was headed. He hoped he would like his new home.

_____

3. I sat down at my desk. I was in big trouble. I did my math homework last night. I put my paper in my backpack. But I did not zip my backpack all the way. On the way to school, a big bird landed on my head! He flew off with my paper. How will I tell Mr. Davis?

_____

Name _____

Marcy visited four stores. Look at the items she bought at each store. Choose the name for each store from the Word Bank.

• •

Word Bank

Grocery Store   Pet Store   Book Store   Toy Store

First Store _____

Second Store _____

Third Store _____

Fourth Store _____

Where would Marcy find all of these stores? Circle the best setting for her shopping trip.

a park   a mall   a farm

Story Elements • CD-104556

Marcy's Shopping Trip (cont.)

Think about the stores that Marcy visited. Describe each setting in a sentence.

Book Store

_____

_____

Grocery Store

_____

_____

Pet Store

_____

_____

Toy Store

_____

_____

Try this: On another sheet of paper write a story about Marcy's shopping trip.

Name _____

When stories are about real places, you can find their settings on a map.
Follow the directions below.

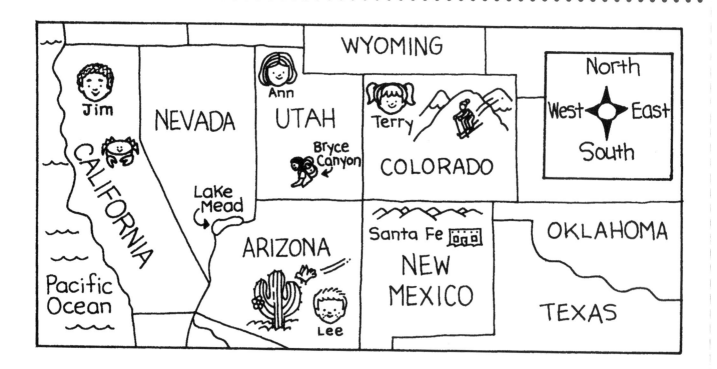

1. Color the state where Ann lives blue.

2. Color the state where Lee lives red.

3. Color the state where Jim lives green.

4. Color the state where Terry lives purple.

5. Color the other states yellow.

Try this: On another sheet of paper write a story.
Draw a map that shows where your story happened.

Name _____

Friends on the Map (cont.)

Four children wrote stories about their friends. Read the stories. Look for clues. Use the map on page 26 to answer the questions.

• •

1. Terry's Friend

One hot day, my friend walked to the beach. He waded into the water. Then he yelled, "Ouch!" A little crab pinched his big toe.

What is the setting?

_____

Who is Terry's friend?

_____

2. Lee's Friend

My friend put on hiking boots and filled a water bottle. She and her mom hiked into Bryce Canyon to see the pretty rocks.

What is the setting?

_____

Who is Lee's friend?

_____

3. Jim's Friend

My friend has a special plant in his backyard. It is a huge cactus. It has big arms. Lots of birds make nests in the arms. My friend likes to watch the birds.

What is the setting?

_____

Who is Jim's friend?

_____

4. Ann's Friend

My friend's vacation was fun. She learned to snowboard. Her family drove to the mountains. It was cold. There was a lot of snow. She learned to slide down the hills.

What is the setting?

_____

Who is Ann's friend?

_____

Science Poster

After a class trip to a space center, Tony and Jeff made a science poster. Read the story about how they made their poster. Circle answers to the questions below.

• •

First, Tony punched holes in black paper. Jeff drew a big circle on white paper and cut it out. It looked just like a full moon. Tony glued his black paper on another piece of white paper. Now, the holes looked like stars in a night sky.

Next, Jeff glued his white paper circle on the black paper. Then, Jeff found a picture of a telescope in a magazine. Tony cut the picture out. He glued it to their poster.

Tony and Jeff were proud of their poster. They showed it to their teacher. Mr. Chan thought their poster looked great. He hung it up in the classroom for everyone to see.

1. What is the best title for the boys' poster?

    Star Watching   Art Day   Trips Are Fun

2. What setting did the boys make?

    a starry night   a classroom   a school bus

3. What did the students do on the trip?

    learned about stars and the moon   hunted for rocks

4. What science equipment did they include on their poster?

    a microscope   a telescope   a magnifying glass

Try this: On another sheet of paper make a poster like the one in the story.

Name_____

Characters in stories have **problems** to solve. Think about these three problems. Use one of them to write a short story below. Make sure your story has an ending that fixes the problem.

• •

A wants a new , but his mom says no.

A wants an 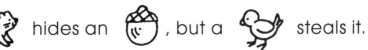 , but she lost her money.

A hides an , but a steals it.

_____

_____

_____

_____

_____

Try this: On another sheet of paper draw a picture of the problem in "Mary Had a Little Lamb."

Name _____

Look at the story. Circle the answer to each question.

1. What is the character?

   a dog   a bone

2. What does the character want?

   to catch a fish   to get a bigger bone

3. What happens at the end of the story?

   He loses his bone.   He gets scared of water.

Beach Trouble

Polly Packrat is having a bad day at the beach. Help Polly get home. Write the letter for each thing that happens next to its picture in the maze.

a. tripped on a rock   b. sunburned her nose

c. bitten by a crab   d. lost her beach ball

e. at home

Try this: On another sheet of paper write a short story that tells about one of Polly's problems.

Mrs. Freeman's Farm

Read the story. Answer the questions on Page 33.

• •

Mrs. Freeman went walking on her farm. She saw Sheep. "How are you today, Sheep?" she asked.

"*Baa-aaa-aad,*" said Sheep. "I am hot and the flies bother me."

Sheep wore a thick coat of hair called wool. Mrs. Freeman shaved the wool from Sheep.

"That feels much better," said Sheep.

"Thank you, Sheep. I will use this wool to make a warm sweater," Mrs. Freeman said.

Mrs. Freeman walked to the barn. She saw Hen outside. "How are you today, Hen?" she asked.

"Not well at all!" said Hen. "Bat is in the barn, and Bat scares me."

"Maybe I can talk Bat into leaving," said Mrs. Freeman.

Mrs. Freeman left. She came back later with a box. "Bat, would you like this new house? I will hang it in a tree by the sheep pen."

Bat looked at the box. "A brand new house for me? Thank you."

Hen was happy. She gave Mrs. Freeman an egg for her breakfast.

Mrs. Freeman was happy too. She loved all the animals on her farm.

Try this: On a separate sheet of paper draw a picture of Mrs. Freeman's farm.

Mrs. Freeman's Farm (cont.)

Look at the different events that happened in the story.
Number them from 1 to 6 to put them in the correct order.

• •

_____ a. Mrs. Freeman had a talk with Hen.

_____ b. Mrs. Freeman shaved wool from Sheep.

_____ c. Mrs. Freeman had a talk with Sheep.

_____ d. Mrs. Freeman got an egg from Hen.

_____ e. Mrs. Freeman went walking on her farm.

_____ f. Mrs. Freeman gave Bat a new home.

The Wrong Picture

Look at the books. The titles tell about each character's problem.
Draw an **X** on the picture that does not match the book.

Try this: On another sheet of paper write a short story that tells about one of the problems.

Name _____

Write the letters on the lines to match each story to its picture.

• •

1. John got a leash. He wanted to take his brand-new puppy for a walk. As John walked to the yard, he cried, "Oh, no!" His sister Josie had taken the puppy out already. _____

2. John pulled on his boots, mittens, and hat. He got his sled and walked to the top of the hill. He looked at the hill. "Oh, no!" he sighed. _____

3. Buster was very hungry. He had played ball with John all morning. He ran to his food bowl. "Oh, no!" panted the puppy. Time to call out for some food! _____

4. Mom wanted to cook eggs for breakfast. She took the carton out and set it on the counter. Buster jumped up. The eggs fell. "Oh, no!" cried Mom. _____

A Gift for Mother

Read the story. Answer the questions below.

• •

Polly the Packrat was alone in her room. She was feeling sad. She wanted to buy her mother a gift. But Polly did not have any money in her toy bank. Polly sat down on her bed. What could she do?

Then Polly smiled and hopped up. She pulled a big bag from under her bed. It held all of her favorite things. Maybe she could use some of them to make a gift.

This is what Polly took out of her bag:

　　　three green buttons　　　one blue feather

　　　one red ribbon　　　　　one brown hat

Polly went to work, and soon she had a surprise for Mother.

1.　Who is the main character? _____

2.　What is her problem? _____

3.　What is the story's setting? _____

4.　Color the picture that shows what Polly made to solve her problem.

Who Is Lost?

Read the story. Answer the questions.

• •

Shauna looked into her pet's bed. Henry should have been fast asleep. Shauna did not see him. Henry was gone! Where did he go?

Shauna looked all around the room. She looked on the floor. She looked in the closet. She looked under her bed. She could not find Henry.

Shauna felt like crying as she got dressed for school. She reached into an open dresser drawer to pull out a shirt. She touched something soft and furry. Then she heard a purr. A tongue licked her fingers. Can you guess what was in Shauna's dresser drawer?

1. Who are the characters? _____

2. What is Shauna's problem? _____

3. Where does this story take place? _____

4. What did Shauna find in her dresser drawer? _____

5. Circle Henry:

Try this: On another sheet of paper, write a paragraph to tell what happens next in the story.

The Cat and the Mice

Read the story. Answer the questions on page 39.

Every day, Kitty Cat chased the mice. She liked to tickle them. But the mice didn't want to be tickled. It made them laugh too much! So, the mice hid inside a hole.

"What can we do?" asked Mother Mouse. "The cat likes to tickle us too much."

"I don't know," said Father Mouse.

"I don't know," said Jimmy Mouse.

"I don't know," said Ramon Mouse.

"I know," said Maria Mouse. "Let's hang a bell around Kitty's neck. Then when we hear her coming, we can run."

Everyone cheered. They told Maria Mouse how smart she was.

Then Ramon Mouse said, "That is a good idea, but we still have a problem. Who will put the bell on the cat?"

The Cat and the Mice (cont.)

Think about the big problem the mice had. Circle the answer to each question.

1. Who are the characters in the story?

   five mice and a cat   five cats   five mice and a dog

2. What is the setting?

   in a school   in a hole   in the forest

3. What is the problem at the beginning of the story?

   The cat laughs at the mice.   The cat tickles the mice too much.

4. What character asks, "What can we do?"

   Maria Mouse   Mother Mouse   Ramon Mouse

5. What character says, "I know"?

   Maria Mouse   Father Mouse   Jimmy Mouse

6. What is the problem at the end of the story?

   Who will look for food?

   Who will put the bell on the cat?

   Who can tickle the cat?

The Snowman

Read the story. Circle key words that describe each setting. List them in the chart below.

• •

Bess lives in Arizona. It is so hot there, it almost never snows. Her best friend, Tyler, just moved to Michigan. Each winter, it gets cold and snows a lot. When the first snow of the season fell, Tyler was excited. He went outside to build his first snowman.

Tyler wrote to Bess and told her how he built his snowman. First, he rolled a big snowball. Then, he made a smaller one and set it on top. Next, Tyler found two dark pebbles on the ground. He used them to make the eyes. He put his dad's fishing hat on top.

Bess wanted to make a snowman too. But how could she do it without snow? She had an idea. She put on her mother's work gloves. Then, she picked up a big ball of tumbleweed. Tumbleweeds are like dry bushes. Bess put a smaller ball of tumbleweed on top. Next, she found two dark pebbles on the ground. She used them for eyes. Then, she got a potato and her brother's cowboy hat. Bess used the potato for a mouth. Then, she put her brother's hat on top.

Bess wrote a letter to Tyler. She told him about her snowman that would never melt!

Bess's Home	Tyler's Home

Name _____

What Happens Next?

Read the stories. Draw what you think happens next.

• •

1. Today is the day of the big base-
ball game. The score is tied. Jenna
needs to hit a home run for her team
to win. She is ready. The pitcher
throws the ball. What happens next?

2. It is a bright, sunny day. Luke and
his parents walk to the dog park.
Luke's puppy, Spot, has his red ball.
What happens next?

┌ ── ── ── ── ── ── ── ── ── ── ── ── ── ┐
Try this: Circle the words that helped you draw the pictures.
└ ── ── ── ── ── ── ── ── ── ── ── ── ── ┘

What Makes a Good Story?

Stories are about **characters.** The place and the time of a story is the **setting.**

Characters usually have **problems** to solve. When characters try to solve their problems, things happen. Those things make up the **plot.**

A plot usually has three parts: the **beginning,** the **middle,** and the **end.**

The **beginning** of a story tells about the characters, the setting, and the problem.

The **middle** of the story tells how the characters try to solve the problem. Sometimes, the characters try two or three things that do not work before finding the right answer.

The **end** of the story tells how the characters finally solve the problem.

When you put all of these different things together, you have a story!

What Makes a Good Story? (cont.)

Look at three stories. Label the **beginning**, the **middle**, and the **end** picture of each plot.

1.

_____ _____ _____

2.

_____ _____ _____

3.

_____ _____ _____

43

Casey the Cowgirl

Read the story. Answer the questions on the next page.

• •

Every morning, Casey puts on her jeans, boots, and cowboy hat. She wants to be a cowgirl like her Aunt Jessie. But she does not have a horse to ride. She tried to ride Bowser, the family's Great Dane. He just sat down. Casey slid off. Then Casey got on the back of the couch. She whooped and yelled until Mom came in.

"Get off the couch and be quiet," she said.

"I am a cowgirl riding my horse, just like Aunt Jessie," Casey said.

Then Casey tried her roping. She did not have any cows to rope, so she tried to rope her stuffed bear. She knocked over a lamp. It broke into pieces. Mom ran in to see what happened.

"Go to your room," she said.

"How will I ever learn to be a cowgirl like Aunt Jessie?" Casey asked.

The next week, Mom said, "I have a surprise. We are going out west to see Aunt Jessie."

"Great!" Casey said. "Now I can learn to be a real cowgirl with real horses and real cows, just like Aunt Jessie!"

Name _____

Casey the Cowgirl (cont.)

Answer the questions about the story on page 44.

· ·

1. Who is the main character? _____

2. What is the setting? _____

3. What is Casey's problem? _____

4. What happened first? _____

    _____

    _____

5. What happened second? _____

    _____

    _____

6. How did the story end? _____

    _____

    _____

7. Would you like to be Casey's friend? Why or why not? _____

    _____

    _____

The End

Read the beginning and middle of each story. Write your own ending.

• •

1. Hoppy Hare and Tommy Tortoise lined up for the start of the race. Hoppy ran and ran. He was far ahead of Tommy, so he sat down under a tree to take a nap.

    What happened? _____

    _____

    _____

2. A crow stole a piece of cheese from a picnic. She flew up in a tree to eat it. A hungry fox saw the crow. He wanted her cheese. He called to the crow, "Oh, pretty crow! Your feathers are shiny. If your voice is sweet too, then you must be a queen." The crow was tricked by the fox. She started to sing.

    What happened? _____

    _____

    _____

3. A boy tending the village sheep got bored. He wanted to play a trick. "Wolf, wolf!" he shouted. All of the people in his village came running. They found the sheep safe and the boy laughing. The next day the same thing happened.

    What happened? _____

    _____

    _____

Answer Key

Page 4
1. three bears and a girl; 2. a woman; 3. a girl and a wolf

Page 5
1. sad face; 2. happy face; 3. happy face; 4. sad face; 5. happy face (kids); sad face (dog); 6. happy face

Page 6
Circle: 1. Lisa; 2. Mark; 3. Ruff; Underline: 1. Lisa Makes a Mask; 2. Mark Flies a Kite; 3. Ruff Finds a Bone

Page 7
Circle: 1. girl; 2. boy; 3. girl; 4. girl; 5. boy

Page 8
1. Gingerbread Man; 2. Itsy Bitsy Spider; 3. Little Red Hen; 4. Baby Bear

Page 9
The titles should match the pictures. Sample responses: 2. Baby Takes a Nap; 3. Paul Runs a Race; 4. Sammy at the Park

Page 10
Answers will vary but should include: 1. a baby fox, a kit; 2. the woods, a den; 3. to go hunting.

Page 11
Answers will vary but should include: 1. a baby cat, a kitten; 2. a house; 3. her family.

Page 12
1. Chan; 2. Pedro; 3. Mary; 4. Keesha; 5. Ted

Page 13
Circle: 1. dog; 2. boy; 3. girl

Pages 14–15
1. animals; 2. make-believe; 3. Marta; 4. Leo; 5. He needed help. 6. She said she would help the lion. Lion: big, roars, big paws; Mouse: small, squeaks, tiny paws

Page 16
1. Circle: castle; 2. Box: cave; 3. Crossout: nest; 4. Underline: playground

Page 17
Answers will vary. Appropriate settings should be drawn around characters.

Page 18
Happy: campfire; castle; beach scene; mother with cookies; Sad: cat in tree; abandoned house, ripped toy; melting snowman

Page 19
Crossout: 1. cow; 2. dinosaur; 3. horse; 4. bathtub; 5. tree

Page 20
1. ball, water, towel; 2. bats, gate, weeds; 3. ice, trees, snow; 4. planets, rocket, stars

Page 21
a. February; b. January; c. November; d. May; e. July; f. October

Page 22
1. Long Ago; 2. Today; 3. Future; 4. Long Ago; 5. Today

Page 23
1. forest; 2. outer space; 3. school

Page 24
First Store: Grocery Store; Second Store: Toy Store; Third Store: Book Store; Fourth Store: Pet Store; Circle: mall

Page 25
Answers will vary. Responses should include a complete sentence that accurately describes each setting.

Page 26
Color: 1. Utah, blue; 2. Arizona, red;
3. California, green; 4. Colorado, purple;
5. Wyoming, New Mexico, Nevada,
Oklahoma, and Texas, yellow

Page 27
1. California; Jim 2. Utah; Ann
3. Arizona; Lee 4. Colorado; Terry. It is also
acceptable to name the physical area
(beach, canyon, etc.).

Page 28
Circle: 1. Star Watching; 2. a starry night;
3. learned about stars and the moon;
4. a telescope

Page 29
Answers will vary. Responses should be
based on one of the three examples and
include a conclusion that solves the main
story problem.

Page 30
1. a dog; 2. to get a bigger bone; 3. He
loses his bone.

Page 31
Order in maze: d; a; c; b; e.

Pages 32–33
A. 4; B. 3; C. 2; D. 6; E. 1; F. 5;

Page 34
Crossout: 1. pancake-flipping fox; 2. clown
with balloons; 3. girl with sleeping puppy;
4. boy at school desk

Page 35
1. d; 2. b; 3. a; 4. c.

Page 36
1. Polly; 2. no money for a gift; 3. Polly's
room; 4. Color: middle picture (hat)

Page 37
1. Shauna and Henry; 2. Henry is missing.
3. Shauna's room; 4. Henry; 5. Circle: cat. It
is also acceptable to call Henry a cat in 1,
2, and 4.

Pages 38–39
Circle: 1. five mice and a cat; 2. in a hole;
3. The cat tickles the mice too much.
4. Mother Mouse; 5. Maria Mouse; 6. Who
will put the bell on the cat?

Page 40
Bess's Home: hot, never snows,
tumbleweed, dark pebbles on the ground;
Tyler's Home: cold, snows a lot, snowballs,
dark pebbles on the ground

Page 41
Pictures will vary, but should show what
could happen next in each story.

Pages 42–43
1. middle, beginning, end; 2. middle, end,
beginning; 3. beginning, middle, end.

Pages 44–45
1. Casey; 2. Casey's house; 3. She wants to
be a cowgirl. Sample responses: 4. Casey
puts on cowgirl clothes, Casey tries to
ride Bowser, Casey uses the couch as a
horse. 5. Bowser sits down/Casey slides off
uses the couch as a horse, Casey tries to
rope her stuffed bear, Casey knocks over
a lamp. 6. The family will visit Aunt Jessie
in Arizona. Casey will be able to ride real
horses. 7. Answers will vary.

Page 46
Sample responses: 1. Tommy wins the race.
2. The crow drops the cheese, and the
fox eats it. 3. When a wolf really comes,
nobody runs when the boy cries, "Wolf!"

Story Elements • CD-104556